To Fall
or To Fly

A POETRY BOOK ON LIFE, LOVE AND TIME.
WRITTEN AND ILLUSTRATED BY SOPHIE BROWN

AuthorHouse™ UK
1663 Liberty Drive
Bloomington, IN 47403 USA
www.authorhouse.co.uk
UK TFN: 0800 0148641 (Toll Free inside the UK)
UK Local: 02036 956322 (+44 20 3695 6322 from outside the UK)

Because of the dynamic nature of the Internet, any web addresses or links contained in this book may have changed since publication and may no longer be valid. The views expressed in this work are solely those of the author and do not necessarily reflect the views of the publisher, and the publisher hereby disclaims any responsibility for them.

This book is printed on acid-free paper.

ISBN: 979-8-8230-8482-6 (sc)
ISBN: 979-8-8230-8483-3 (e)

Library of Congress Control Number: 2023917981

Print information available on the last page.

Published by AuthorHouse 01/29/2024

authorHOUSE®

Contents

Chapter 4:   Algea – Bringer of Pain

Chapter 5:   Hermes – See the World

Chapter 1:

CHRONOS – TIME ITSELF

The Flash of Time

Time is the relentless river that no one can slow,
dazzling with splashes of happiness,
then gone before you know.

Rushing rapids that leave you gasping out of breath,
clutching at dripping water, now there's no time left.

a story amongst us,
or a story without.

Time's fleeting gift you try not to forget,
hoping the waterfall won't taste of regret.
a heavy dream too vivid to be true,
left with only Chronos,
and you.

May

A rush of wind and the petals dance like falling snow,
White and pink in the twilight they glow,

In an infinite spiral they twirl,
bowing and spinning in a perfect curl.

The wind rushes through the chestnut trees,
dark hair dancing in the brisk breeze.

Then the air sits still
and the petals fall,
   upon the hill

Spring confetti on a windy day,
Celebrating the beauty of May

The Willow Tree of Life

Under the great willow tree,
Among the strands of vitality,
Death and life dance across the ivory sands of time,
Their bare feet kicking glowing dust into the nights sky.

Death kisses her cheek and takes her hand,
under their dance our future's planned,
She bursts of moments her dress full of desired dreams,
Pinned together with poverty's broken seams.

Because we are all willow leaves
Brushing the air with wistful sighs.
Some of us intertwined,
until another dies,
And Death catches the falling soul,
To replant it in the ground,
Because life never truly ends,
They are always around.

In the birds soaring through the sky,
And the travellers who wander the land,
In the kids left behind,
And in those who still stand.

And Life and Death lie down together to observe the world with love,
They both cry in sadness for the moments they will miss,
But also cry in joy for those moments filled with bliss.

Ready or Not Here I Come

One, two.
We sprinkled the glitter of time across the promised space,
And danced in the blissful lights of a smiling face.
Laughs were not plastered like walls, but raging in joy,
A picnic of paintings in a world shaped like a toy.

Three, four.
Monsters migrate from under the bed to our reflection,
And the dark is without love but screams for a connection.
Instead confined to a multitude of blankets we hide,
As the flower of naivety slowly wilts inside.

Five, six.
Gnarled sticks like deformed wands are clutched in fists,
From playing to praying, now the demons exist,
We built our castle and with it came the dragon to fight,
Reaching for the top with childish cries of might.

Seven, eight.
As bees we are stuck in a tiresome routine,
Slaves within a sticky mess of our own vicious queen.
We are merely specks within the swarm fooling ourselves we pretend,
Our sting is freedoms key and not our imminent end.

Nine, ten.
The radiance from our desk lamp is now our only source of light.
As we form reckless piles of money in greedy spitc.
Heaving our bodies into baths of vodka and gold,
Shuddering with shallow breaths in a hope we still have a soul.
    -Now that we are old

Star Gazing

The stars gazed at me,
like an array of shinning faces.
I wonder what they see,
in earths forgotten places.

I feel like a ghost caught backstage,
a bird that couldn't fly,
a writer without a page,
a river running dry.

I'm the most important nothing,
the most significant insignificance,
in existence.

Yet still on this carpet of grass I lie,
as the stars gaze at me from up in the night sky.

The memory of the Sun

It whispers across my frozen lips,
Nostalgia painted by a child's fingertips.
Glowing light reflects off tear filled eyes,
Hazy yet bright, unburdened by lies.
And the soft innocence of unnoticed flaws,
The blissful ignorance of closed doors.
Women made 'children' again.
Until
    we
        fell
And hands once filled with toys now shake with desire,
Anxiety' tremor like a kestrel flying higher,
And the silence they shouted brought a storm,
The baby blue paintings ripped and torn.

Drops slid down broken memories,
Drops slid down burning cheeks.
The strings of youth undone
Left only with,

The memory of the Sun.

<u>River of life</u>

I have spent my whole life in a race,
pulled d
       o
         w
           n stream by the rushing water of time,
longing for a brighter future without life's stress,
looking to tomorrow and not seeing today,
washing away years for the sake of success.

First, I couldn't wait to finish school, then to end work and retire,
Ignoring the burning light of life's fire,
But not once did I stop and enjoy where I was at that time, on that day,
So, when the surging river began to fade, I would say-

"That I longed to turn back. But a river only goes one way."

Chapter 2:

EROS – WORDS OF LOVE

Eros

Bursting forth he blazes like meteors,
in fields of tranquillity.
Over romantic rivers he soars,
striding into infinity.

More than atoms he's something beautiful,
this spark of love that makes lust so dutiful.
To reveal the love dust like a lamp in a haze,
on he goes to blaze, and blaze.

Dust that enlightens the sightless
caught in beams of his brightness.
So, pull tight the curtain of loss,
and blaze, blaze the longing arrows of
- Eros

Love or Lust

I'm caught with mis-objection,
pulled by desire with no direction.
I'm lost in the sweeping cliffs of my ambition,
coiled in a snake of indecision.
Following rivers of romance into celestial spheres,
galaxies of moments twinkling over the years,
but the rivers end in waterfalls,
jump to fly we risk it all.
And I'm dancing over the story line like skipping across a tightrope,
gathering scattered moments of hope,
to fold beneath the sun's colossal kiss,
embracing oblivion in the creative abyss.

Am I the aurora amidst this cosmic night,
dancing through life's pleasurable streams?
or the one who comes home to a warm light,
to peace, care, and the partner of my dreams.

True Love

Being 'in love' is a temporary feeling,
It's the hearts vaccine a new way of healing.
It erupts like the blossom in spring to then fall away...
Leaving you lost in the fog to find your own way.

But in that haze, you may discover.
God's gift of 'true love' inside another.
When your roots delve so deep, they join together,
And you're standing tall despite the weather.

'True Love' is the song of the deaf, it's the art of the blind:
It's not breathless, it's not breaking, it binds.
And so here we are witness to a love I believe is 'true'.
Celebrating those before us
Now as one. Not two.

Bitter Ache

To whisper into the darkness and know there's no one there.
No force of comfort.
Now my head high on two pillows,
holds toxic thoughts rising like bubbling gas,
erupting in the dark water.
To turn my back,
but on what?
The wall is my cold new companion,
-it hugs me roughly

I wish to part the beds, but fear I will roll off the edge,
like a lost traveller reaching the ends of the earth,
for the futile hope of love and worth.

Oh, how my bitter heart aches for you to be near,
for your voice in my ear,
tears fell as I wept.
on the right side of the bed where you once slept.

Hot Air of Summers Love

My heart breaks for you over this lapping lake,
An ache that swallows me like the setting sun,
and I'm lost amongst high peaks of desire,
While bright future lights glitter across the water,
marred in the mirage,
a rippling reflection,
of time to come.
The shrinking moon is now a slither of a smile,
lying on the hot air of summers love,
Wrap me in this sunset safe in your arms,
and constellations will sing above the light,
as the sun closes her tired eyes,
to embrace the blissful, calm of night.

My murderer called love.

Explosives are wrapped around my chest, the fuse between my teeth.
And I told you to run, because when I explode, I didn't want to see you bleed...
No way I can be defused.
Instead, I am reduced,
Reused,
Recycled,
Like bits of trash
Torn up cash,
- I once held so much value but now my heart is ticking
Run. It's not a lullaby,
Go! You have to say goodbye.
Clutched tight in your fist is the lighter
Tick, Hide from me!

Tick. Don't see the way my eyes beg you to stay when I whisper for you
to leave.
Tick. Don't smell the way I'm emotionally leaking like a broken machine.
Tick. Don't hear the count down in my heart or listen to me scream,
Don't tell me I'm being extreme,
Run outside and lock the door.
Just another casualty in this war.

You look at me with pity buried deep,
Eyes wet as you weep,
-Like this wasn't what you wanted
-Like you didn't mean to steal my heart and replace it with this bomb
that it was someone else's wrong.
Drip, the heart in your hand is crying blood.
Drip, the crimson colour seeps deep into the mud.
It's crazy how you did this to me, but I still want to save you...
It's stupid that although you're my murderer I still want to act brave
for you.
I fell into my murderer willing with trust and not with a shove,
Never seeming to notice my murderer always had the same name: 'Love'

Chapter 3:

OIKOS – INTO SOCIETY

Oikos

We rolled the ball of time,
and watched the seasons fade,
the light and dark of each passing day.

we balanced scales to find what is right,
and scattered souls across the starry night,
We tunnelled through mountains, tamed the seas,
taught birds to sing and befriended the bees.

We pulled homes out of the earth,
to fill with people made from star dust,
then sparked the fires of lust,
to see the golden light of birth.

Science VS Religion

Our lab coats and crosses we wear like labels.
Spreading our cards out on the table,
we have split our hand.
And like fuel to a fire, tensions rising higher,
Our myths- now historical accounts
Our knowledge – the new revelation
Stop.
Listen to the church bells and how they battle with theories.
The chimes of time
A crescendo of conflict none can miss!
Is it ignorance or bliss?
Battles against rights,
Going against commandments to fight
Each hypocrite bigger than the last...
To embrace the future is to sacrifice the past.
Confusion mixed on earth's face,
Continents colliding into a frown.
The nations of hope start to drown,
Burning houses call the smell,
Grandparents whisper to children, "only time can tell. Just be ready for
the coming of the bells".
Men who can't see, lead the blind into the night,
As sinners are exalted in windows of light,
Time won't tell, there's no decision,
Here lies the conflict of Evolution vs Religion.

Man Up

Men are told to man up,
Like every problem can be solved by "growing a pair",
You can't punch your way out of emotions, arm wrestle with depression,
By saying this are you questioning the amount of masculinity a person owns,
To check their wardrobes and make sure it's all blue,
Because I thought you knew
Pink is only for girls,
And purple.... Well, there's no such thing.

Never have I heard "women up" this suggests being brave,
Is saved just for guys,
And we drink in these stereo typical lies,
Like that beer at the pub labelled "way out of problem".
Cowards. That's the sort of person who tells you to "man up" because they can't face problems with open eyes,
No, they need to go in with guns in hand,
shoot and ask questions later is always the plan.
Women inferior are like props in a play where all the men are heroes,
In a quest to conquer... Feelings.

Someone once told me that we are all just bricks keeping up a haunted house.
And although we don't let the roof fall
Together big and alone small.
Inside we share
this evil air,
But be aware,
you can't be scared,
Just! "Grow a pair"

Never take off the weight resting on your shoulders...
If you are struggling you clearly need to go back to the gym,
Because muscles can hold up the clouds
Hold off the crowds,
-Of people who want to help and talk about more than sex and cars.

How many more boys need to kill themselves for the world to realise
they are not made of metal?
To look after girls that are formed into these petals,
Girls smell so sweet that when they cry, they are just watering their own
roots to grow up to the sky,
But boys don't cry.
And when a man sheds a tear
All it shows,
Is how fear in a man proves he's rusting, peeling,
Needing to be polished of these: time wasting, messy, disgusting,
inconvenient- feelings.

So, the next time my friends when someone tells you to "man up".
Turn and go,
But not before telling them-

"no"

Life's reflection

The rippling reflection of the sky stares at me,
Its scattered clouds glow as the sun dives into the sea. Moments, fleeting,
like the wisps of life that pass me by
The muddled reality on the wet deck slaps into the sky,
And I imagine a person's life, their experiences displayed on the wooden
panels,
When life is just the distance you travel before you fall off the edge
   Of the reflexion

Refugees

We lost everything,
The huddled bodies of gnarled limbs, lie,
-abandoned, unwanted like rats
swarming flies
Echoing cries...

We lost everything,
Sun glares on burnt, beaten backs,
Our problem the horizon that's stalking,
A defeated nation left with nothing but walking.

"Open your doors! Your mind is a locked cell of ignorance",
We were stripped of dignity,
Tripped in others greed for victory,
Left on our knee's hands joined in prayer,
Daring you to look us in our eyes to tell us "You don't care".

We lost everything,
Ripped from our reality,
Just another civilian fatality.
Your place or mine? For who will suffer?
What is humanity with no love for one another?

We cry.
We smile.
We laugh.

The refugees
Not selfish thieves
We are no different from you.
We are humans! And we lost...

Everything.

Drifting

Call me confused,
Call me lost,
I'm pollen caught in the fingers of the wind,
I'm the plea,
drifting in a bottle at sea.
A paradox of feelings
In this vault I am free.
I'm the oxymoron of life,
the middle of the sentence.

Call me numb.
Call me careless,
I've reached a place of unawareness.
Drowning in routine
-Caught in the crevice of a smile,
In the witness of tears
Living in a memory of a thousand years...
Yesterday is now and now is already too late,
Drifting my conscious is pulled by the tides of fate.

Our society

The white glowing light of your screen,
poised breathlessly over pornography,
your life a ceaseless darkness blazed for a brief second by a spark of
adrenaline.

Fumbling in the monotonous routine,
mind screaming profanities so obscene,
in the dull grey silence that seems to rake the roaring wind of this earth,
hair lashing around one's face from birth,
like the ties of society holding on to your ambition,
trapping you inside a vault of submission.

The darkness of the crowd,
their heads taller and taller expectations rising higher,
as your wait for the fire,
calculated and ready for the moment you will see the light,
this longed-for moment of realisation.

When redemption meets enlightenment in a shining euphoric rupture
of applause,
and in the applause, you begin to sink into your narcissistic soul,
like a condemned, corpse's coffin as it falls to be burned.
down to where you first received your life,

from those very ashes
now resembling the burnt end of a cigarette,
crack filled nostrils and alcohol-soaked blood,
left only with the blaze of your fire,
and the ashes of our society's broken desire.

Chapter 4:

ALGEA – BRINGER OF PAIN

Algea's Tears

Tears mark the moment Algea comes,
With fright and rage in devil tongues,
Wracked with pain and cold defeat,
Left begging at Algea's feet.

Suffocating souls with endless grief,
This cruel world offers no relief,
Raining flames and suffering heat,
This goddess you do not want to meet.

The Poppy's

The sun casts shadows on the floor friend and foe:
Are the crosses that parade row on row.
The richest wonders lie locked in the graves,
Inventions never spoken, words we cannot save.
Instead to silence they are condemned.
The least we could do is remember them....

The field of Poppy's salute to the sky
Their arms weak with the question of "why?"
As they watch blundering souls tear apart peace where they are laid.
-Would they ask if their sacrifice was well paid?

Do they watch, with shaking heads at, our selfish ways?
Do they play football every Christmas in those peaceful days?
Peering through fogged windows can they still see our smile?
Or is that too like the names engraved washed off after a while…?

In Flanders field they do not sleep. Or dream.
As lovely as that may seem,
-In Flanders field their spirit's roam
Brushing past their friends, in stone.

I'm tired.

I'm tired,
Of waking up traumatised
The torture fills my eyes,
I know it's not real,
But it's all I can feel,
The glass as it cuts my skin,
The hurt as I'm broken from within.
Beaten in my childhood room,
Mauled by dogs and trapped in a tomb,
The fear that makes my heart race,
The sweat pouring on my furrowed face,
I wake up in heaven,
But I always sleep in hell.
There are no words that can tell,
The pain of these dreams,
Sanity fraying at the seams.
I can smell the blood as they cut my neck,
Feel the sting that I want to forget,
The breeze on the roof as I dodge the spears,
Why do I always wake in fear?
When I fall asleep so happy and strong
But now I'm falling,

falling

and I can't fall for long,
I hit the stone and wake up in paradise,
Which reality is real? I must think twice,
I'm tired of holding trapped tears in my eyes,
I'm tired of being traumatised.

Curtains

Curtains keep in treasured moments they evade a stranger's sight,
But also keep hidden rooms of fear and no light.
When you meet me
A pair of curtains you will see.

-Because when I'm bright I'm cold inside...
So often shout to "pull myself together" and that's why I lied!

I shut myself in to keep warm.
Rather than being brave and facing the storm,
I lied that I was busy with books,
When I'm avoiding the 'looks'

Someone once told me 'Eyes are windows to your soul'.
Well, I guess mine are closed...
Because when you meet me
A pair of curtains you will see.

Grief

Like a monster ripping open a whole where my heart is,
The vacuum sucks away my breath
-This suffocating grasp of death.

Eyes of ghosts watch me cry,
As I weep for those who did die
I ask why?
Why does it have to be those so great,
That end up in the graves of fate...
It's a giant bruise so long and sore,
It shakes my body,
to the core

This screaming voice ringing in my ears!
The rain resembles rapid running tears,
And I thought of all those innocent years,
Where I missed saying: "I love him."

Time does pass,
but there's no relief,
For this never ending
Feeling of grief.

Trevor

You played with planes when you were young,
Clenched in your small fist ready to be flung,
Heart full of dreams up in the clouds,
Ready to amaze and dazzle the crowds.

The adventure shone from you wild and free,
And everyone around you could see,
The twinkle in your bright blue eyes,
When you looked up longingly to the sky.

You spread your arms and embraced the day,
Every room brighter from the words you would say,
Reaching closer you hiked into the sun,
Never complaining, but always having fun.

You shined with joy when you learnt to fly,
Finally at one with the celestial blue sky,
Spinning and rolling like a dancing dove,
Free at last and soaring up above.

The more you flew your passion grew,
Your knowledge and your talent too.
To turn legend planes almost lost,
Into flying eagles despite the cost.

You performed to crowds like you always dreamed,
With a loving family your smile beamed,
You taught me to fly drifting above the earth,
Inspiring everyone with adventures worth.

You paid tribute to all the men that had fallen at war,
You sacrificed your life so their memory could soar,
No words can say how you will be missed,
You truly did live and not just exist.

<u>The living dead</u>

Lips once gathered into a smile were now thrown down to sag and slur with his slipping speech,
Hands once strong, tremor, fingers left clasping at broken shards of normality, falling out of reach,

Eyes once bubbling with thoughts are now condemned to plea in shallow sockets for a shred of dignity,
As children watch frozen in the moment of denial as their crumpling father is relapsed into infinity.

Taut ivory skin over frail bones no longer glow with the gift of life, but instead the curse of the living dead.
As the disease takes away even the memory of his own voice, left to an isolation trapped sane inside his head.

Chapter 5:

HERMES – SEE THE WORLD

Adventures of Hermes

To break the clouds and sail the seas,
Jump through jungles of towering trees,
Feel the icy wind and blistering heat,
A world laid out under flying feet.

Searching the world for lost names,
To bring them down the path of flames,
A rushing energy of his divine might,
The traveller Hermes soaring into the light.

The Beach

My toes bury into the wet sand,
the sea's tongue licking at my ankles.
I was speechless,
For this fleeting moment of infinite peace
was cocooned so beautifully into this world of suffering.

The grains of sand that run through my toes are like people,
pulled by the tides of fortune.
Some are beaten into dust,
Yet others form mighty castles in their triumph,

The setting sun reflects off the bubbles like falling glass orbs,
Tumbling into the beach.
As the serenity of the ocean collided with the chaos of
humanity,
And disease clutches like a snake on to moments such as these.

Although the shadow of our destruction creeps up behind me
I too shall hold on:
To this moment
To this beach
and to the soft sand that rests in the palm of my hand.
Because all the little moments of happiness
                        That's what makes up the world.

Sunset drive in Bangkok

Corrugated metal is perched precariously on top of the colourful houses,
They sit drunk in the green undergrowth slanting uniquely.
The air is thick and wet as the setting sun pushes through the curtains of dust,
Overhead trains drift above the chaos,
Their carriages akin to a child's toy.
Behind them spires, from ancient temples, rupture the orange mist,
Their decorative walls glimmer as they catch the fading light.
The old buildings sit proudly amongst their tall neighbours,
Which tower obnoxiously over the city- scraping at the sky,
The sun peaks through the gaps in Bangkok's Forest of stone,
A huge, glowing, deep red orb.
Under the sun's stare, an outside market teems with life,
Stalls piled high with exotic fruits, and jewellery, sit beneath a multicoloured canopy.
I can hear the accumulative hum of the motorbikes, as they surge through the streets in their hundreds,
swerving past tourists, tuk-tuks and neon signs.
Palm trees in regimented lines salute to the building beyond
A peach palace edged in dazzling white rock,
Just a taste of the majesty of Bangkok.

Lost

The branches scratched at my bare legs,
each tree as unfamiliar as the last,
alone and scrambling, through the dirt,
in this forest a universe of green so vast.

Tears run down my face like liquid-crystal,
Deep thoughts bury into my skull,
There is no escape the trees have me trapped,
I feel nothing now everything is dull.

The mask of sweet pine leaves fills my nose,
And the silence my ears
My limbs are weak with fatigue,
And my eyes filled with tears.

I let up smoke they did not see,
I screamed for help they heard no sound,
I left marks on trees they did not notice,
                    I'm not lost. I'm just not found.

Lisbon

I'm stunned by your magnificence scattered with orange roofs,
I'm falling in love with the purple trees,
-Brushing past your cobbled streets.
Twisting alleys whisper of hidden secrets
Gems of tranquillity,
In this bustling city of vitality.

I'm in awe of your lights,
Sparkling along the dark horizon.
The moon glade glimmering upon the yellow trams,
Their deep rhythm keeping the time.
As the water rolls under the wide arms of the sanctity of Christ,
sculpted eyes watching Lisbon with a steady stare.

Your voluptuous orange trees are bursting with fruit,
While white petals dance along the tracks like rolling pearls,

Running to the bridge that hovers proudly in the distance,
It's great arms stretching across your jealous lagoon.
The clouds above are like splashes of paint lit up by the cold moon,
Silhouetted in the sky by the soaring swallows,
And the night is alive with the joy of revellers,
And the faint patter of pedestrians
Their heels clicking upon your mosaic floor.

A breeze brushes past my face,
Your warm spring air holds a promise,
So deep
Of beauty and harmony,
Resting at the coast by your feet.

I watch in awe, at this city of wisdom,
Stunned by the magnificence of beautiful Lisbon.

Tropical Storm

The tropical rain fell,
heavy from the sky,
it pierced the humid air and splashed to the ground,
The swimming pool once smooth now appeared fuzzy as elephant skin,
The din of rainfall drifted over the hotel like a broken radio,
the static noise was low as drops were swallowed into puddles,
high, as it bounced off the roofs.
Amidst the storm the palm trees leaned over sighing in relief,
and grasping at the water with their luscious green leaf's.
Suddenly Gods camera flashed across the white sky,
met by the rumbling applause of thunder.
The deep noise grew louder as we sat in the stomach of the
cosmos,
the smell of wet dusty tiles surging up in the warm air,
where a band of birds laughed sweetly in the sky,
playing in the tropical storm of Chiang Mia.

Drop

Standing on the edge gravity has never been stronger,
Eye lids shutting, seconds have never taken longer,
Knees are weak and legs like simple strings,
Arms are carelessly stretched like a bird's new wings,
The dramatic sky has never looked so frightening,
And the jump into oblivion so inviting.

About the author

I'm a 23-year-old artist, poet, author, and musician living in Bristol. I have won prizes in the Cheltenham literature festival, in slam poetry competitions, and have been selling my paintings for the last four years. Creative expression has been an important passion of mine since the age of 5 when I first started writing poems. Creating has helped me to work through darker days and move to a happier state of mind. My aim is to create poetry to express some of the deep feelings I have had through my life, to give them meaning. I hope that others who can relate to these emotions, realise they are not alone.

'To Fall or To Fly' dives into the beauty and harsh reality of life portrayed through poetry and paintings. It is a raw expression of love and time, conflict, and adventure. The chapters are categorized by the timeless Greek gods who represent the theme of the poems. Part of our language has been derived from these gods, marking their influence as the muses of language and culture. This book takes you on a journey through realms of emotion, exploring the struggles and passions of our mortal lives.

Printed in the United States
by Baker & Taylor Publisher Services